CASSANDRA CLARE

CASSANDRA CLARE

DANIEL E. HARMON

ROSEN
PUBLISHING®

New York

Published in 2015 by The Rosen Publishing Group, Inc.
29 East 21st Street, New York, NY 10010

First Edition

Library of Congress Cataloging-in-Publication Data

Harmon, Daniel E.
Cassandra Clare/Daniel E. Harmon.—First edition.
    pages cm.—(All about the author)
Includes bibliographical references and index.
ISBN 978-1-4777-7912-5 (library bound)
1. Clare, Cassandra—Juvenile literature. 2. Authors, American—20th century—Biography—Juvenile literature. 3. Authors, American—21st century—Biography—Juvenile literature. I. Title.
PS3603.L3518Z66 2015
813'.6—dc23
[B]

2014010965

Manufactured in China

CONTENTS

On the floor of New York City's Pandemonium Club, fifteen-year-old Clary Fray sways to the electronic pulse of trance music. But her mind is on neither the dance nor her companion, Simon. With a strange foreboding, she watches a boy with blue-dyed hair follow a beautiful girl dressed in white through the door of a storeroom marked, "NO ADMITTANCE." Alarmed, she notices two other boys dressed in black slip into the room behind them. One stalker draws a knife as they enter.

Clary urges Simon to alert a security guard while she steals into the storage room to investigate. Her darkest apprehension unfolds. Peering from behind a concrete pillar, she sees the girl in white and the boys in black—conspirators—bind and kill the indigo-haired teen. Confronting them, she is barraged by angry questions. Who is she? What does she know of demons and warlocks? Has she communicated with the Night Children?

Her nightmarish encounter is suddenly interrupted when Simon arrives, accompanied by the club bouncer. To her bewilderment, neither of her allies can see or hear the strange threesome surrounding her—and the victim's body has vanished.

A dream? Not at all. Clary comes to discover she is a mundie (human) who, inexplicably, can see into the inhuman world of demons and the legion of

Shadowhunters dedicated to fight them. As the tale unfolds with dramatic revelations, questions begin to haunt her. Is she a Shadowhunter herself, suddenly coming into her own identity?

Thus begins *City of Bones*, the first book in Cassandra Clare's series of urban fantasy novels for young adult readers titled the Mortal Instruments. Published in 2007, *City of Bones* became an immediate *New York Times* best seller. It was followed over

Cassandra Clare is backed by a poster of her leading characters at the 2013 premiere of *The Mortal Instruments: City of Bones*, the film based on her first book.

the next seven years by five more titles in the series. Meanwhile, Clare began work on a prequel series called the Infernal Devices. Its three books, *Clockwork Angel*, *Clockwork Prince*, and *Clockwork Princess*, are set in London during the late 1800s. All of her books have become tremendously popular among teenagers.

Interestingly, Clare had no early ambitions to become a fiction writer. As a child, however, she read books voraciously. By age twelve, she had begun writing short stories and even novels—all of which, she now reflects, were of terrible quality. College writing courses proved unfulfilling, so she decided to become a magazine journalist instead. For several years she wrote entertainment articles, including features about Hollywood celebrities.

Her career interests took a surprising turn when she got a part-time job at a children's bookstore. She began rereading some of the books she'd loved while growing up, which rekindled her desire to write juvenile fiction. "Most people who love to write," Clare remarks on her website, "start with a love of reading."

Clare's own works are inspiring a generation of future authors. *Kirkus Reviews* called *City of Bones* "a cool, pleasingly dark and spicy urban fantasy." *Publishers Weekly* said the Mortal Instruments series presents "a compelling story about family secrets and coming-of-age identity crises." An Indigo Books review said of *Clockwork Angel*, "It's fun, but more importantly: it's well-written fun."

At this writing, Clare's novels have sold more than twenty-six million copies.

A CHILD OF THE WORLD

I t might seem prophetic that Cassandra Clare was born in Iran, at the geographical center of what once was the Persian Empire. Ancient Persian culture was rich in the arts and is remembered in part for its eloquent poetry and fantastic legends. Classic works include *The Arabian Nights*, a collection of stories featuring such enchanting characters as Aladdin. Little did her parents imagine their daughter one day would create her own fictional characters, who would enchant international young readers of the twenty-first century.

Judith Rumelt (her real name) was born to Richard and Elizabeth Rumelt in Tehran on July 27, 1973. Although

political tensions run high today between Iran and the United States, in 1973, the two nations were allies. Many Americans lived in Iran at that time.

Richard Rumelt is an author and business professor. The family traveled extensively. By the time Cassandra was in her teens, they had lived in England, France, and Switzerland. For a month while she was a toddler, she basically lived inside her father's backpack as they ventured on foot through the Himalaya Mountains.

Westminster Abbey is one of London's most famous historic landmarks. Clare's childhood fascination with Victorian London would ultimately inspire the setting for her second series, the Infernal Devices.

One period of her childhood would have a profound effect on her career. This was when they lived in London, England. While her father worked at the London School of Economics, Cassandra was under the instruction of her mother. They spent much of their time exploring the famous city, especially its history. They visited Buckingham Palace, the Tower of London, and many other famous places.

Cassandra, who was about ten at the time, was fascinated by the stories behind the world-renowned landmarks and especially the history of the royal families. In "Kids' Q&A" for Powell's Books, she recalled a visit with her parents to Westminster Abbey, where many English notables are buried. "My dad started telling me who was buried there, and how they died. I guess he didn't notice I was turning green, because eventually he dragged me over into a corner, pointed at the ground, and said, 'And this is where Mary Queen of Scots is buried . . . *in two pieces.*' At which point I immediately threw up on the floor."

She also became absorbed in period literature, particularly the Sherlock Holmes stories and novels of Arthur Conan Doyle. She has felt strongly attached to London since that time and has returned often.

Clare has been an incessant reader all her life. As a student, her absorption with books sometimes got her into trouble when it distracted her from classroom teaching.

THE QUIET KID IN THE CORNER

Clare is amused that people who know her today are shocked to be told how quiet and reserved she was as a child. She read constantly, carrying a book under her arm almost everywhere she went.

"I was the quiet kid in the corner, reading a book," she told Cynthia Leitich Smith on the *Cynsations* blog. Some of her school-teachers, she confided, forbade her from read-ing during class because she did it constantly. "I've always thought that was something of a counterpro-ductive measure. I mean, shouldn't you want kids to read? Admittedly maybe not during biology class."

She believes her love of reading eventually led to her career as a writer—and that, she assumes, is the way it is with all writers. In "Author Interview: Cassandra Clare" on the *Bookish Type* blog, she explained, "One day you're thinking, 'I really wish I could read a book that had this, and *this*, and *this*,' and then you realize, 'Well, I could always write that book.' You're your own first reader, after all."

Her voracious reading habit has continued throughout her life. Clare agrees with author Stephen King, who suggests reading at least seventy books a year.

A FATHERLY INFLUENCE

Clare says her father has had an enormous influence on her career, not just as a successful author in his own right but also as her business adviser. As a long-time professor at the UCLA Anderson School of Management, Richard Rumelt has written numerous business texts. A *Financial Times* reviewer called his book *Good Strategy/Bad Strategy: The Difference and Why It Matters* "the most interesting business book of 2011."

In a father/daughter interview with *Fortune* magazine's David Kaplan, Clare talked about her father's business savvy. "I grew up listening to him talk about strategy and management. I've read his book, obviously. And he's always pressed upon me that

A STORYTELLING ROLE MODEL

Cassandra Clare's grandfather, Max Rosenberg (1914–2004), was a motion picture producer who specialized in films about horror, the supernatural, and science fiction. Among his more than fifty productions was *The Curse of Frankenstein*, credited as the first horror movie made in color. Other notable films were *Tales from the Crypt* and *The Land That Time Forgot*.

"He was a huge believer in the power of storytelling and always, from when I was a little kid, was giving me fantastic books," she said in an interview with Sophie Schillaci of the *Hollywood Reporter*. Rosenberg was keenly interested in folklore and mythology. Clare acknowledges that much of her grandfather's influence and interests have had a strong effect on her books.

Clare dedicated *City of Bones* to her grandfather. In the interview, "Cassandra Clare, Author Extraordinaire," on the *3 Evil Cousins* blog, she said that if she could spend a day with any one individual living or dead, it would be him. Clare explained, "He died right before I sold the Mortal Instruments and I'd like to be able to tell him how great everything's been going with it."

the person who had a strategy is going to win out over the person who doesn't. So when I come into a [publishing-related] situation, my immediate question is, 'Well, what's the strategy?' And I think that's unusual for a writer."

She and her dad have discussed marketing ideas such as giving away a digital version of the first book in a series. Such a move would broaden reader interest and increase sales of subsequent volumes.

Rumelt teasingly cited "genetics" as the reason his daughter has become an even more widely read author than himself. He genuinely takes great pride in her success.

TRANSITIONING FROM READER TO WRITER

A question Clare is frequently asked—and one that has always baffled her—is at what point she decided to become a writer. Readers seem to sense that "there comes a moment when you know you are a writer, that it's something you're destined to do," she muses on her website. Not so for her. She continues, "I started writing books when I was about twelve . . . I wrote a terrible vampire novel and a terrible mystery novel and a terrible romance novel and a terrible Arthurian novel."

A CLASSIC SHORT NOVEL INSPIRES A PEN NAME

Jane Austen (1775–1817) is one of many famous authors of past centuries whose classic works enthralled young Judith Rumelt. While in her early teens, Austen had penned a short novel about a young Englishwoman setting out to find her way in the world. She titled the piece *The Beautifull Cassandra.* In Greek mythology, Cassandra was a Trojan princess who had prophetic power, but no one believed her. Jane Austen's mother and her older sister, a watercolor painter, both were named Cassandra.

Among Clare's literary influences is classical author Jane Austen. Clare took her pen name from the title of one of Austen's early novels, *The Beautifull Cassandra.*

Two centuries later, a teenaged Judith Rumelt wrote a short novel of her own and used Austen's title for it. When in adulthood she made writing her profession, she was drawn to the name of the central character. Thus, most readers today know Rumelt by her pen name: Cassandra Clare.

While in high school in Los Angeles, her dabbling included short stories, which she wrote mainly for her friends, and the novel she titled *The Beautiful Cassandra.* She was inspired to write it by a short novel with a similar title written by Jane Austen.

MYTHOLOGY AND FANTASY FOR FUN AND PROFIT

Throughout her life, Clare has been especially interested in ancient mythology and folk tales. As a child, she found it an absorbing literary genre from her viewpoint as a reader. Now an author, she has made it a focus of her career.

Years of reading and research into the mythology of different world cultures are behind her best selling fantasy series. Two literary classics, *Paradise Lost* and Dante's *Inferno*, provide keystones for her overall concept. *Paradise Lost*, published in 1667, is John Milton's epic poem about Adam and Eve and the fall of mankind at the hands of Satan. *The Inferno* (early fourteenth century), part of *The Divine Comedy* trilogy, is Dante Alighieri's poetic vision of a journey through hell.

But Clare wanted to encompass mythology from around the world, not just Europe. "So I did a lot of reading up on world mythology, especially anything having to do with good and evil spirits," she tells

This nineteenth-century painting depicts the conquest of Satan in John Milton's *Paradise Lost*. The eternal clash between good and evil is an underlying theme in Clare's books.

visitors to her website. "I wanted to make sure multiple types of demonic myth were present, so you'll find Japanese, Indian, Tibetan, and other kinds of demons represented (plus the kind I've made up). I read a lot of old 'demonologies' . . . I read up on the mythology of angels and fallen angels."

Eventually, she would create a supernatural world championed by Nephilim, who in ancient mythology were the offspring of angels and humans. Before she began devoting herself to fantasy fiction, though, she cut her teeth on a form of nonfiction reporting: entertainment journalism.

FROM TAB JOURNALISM TO FANTASY FICTION

C lare took writing courses in college but was not particularly motivated by them. The experience caused her to think perhaps fiction writing wasn't for her.

Her college major was English. On her website, she tells aspiring writers that majoring in English is not required for them to realize their ambitions: "There are no school or educational requirements for becoming a writer, though you can always choose to take classes if you want to. Mostly what I did that was significant was read a great deal."

CELEBRITY CHASING AND CHILDREN'S BOOKS

As a student, Clare was unsure what career she wanted to pursue. With college

Before she became a full-time novelist, Clare worked as an entertainment writer for such popular periodicals as the *Hollywood Reporter*.

behind her, she began two jobs—completely different, it may have seemed at the time, but their connection would become more obvious in the long run. Her main occupation was in the entertainment media as a writer and editor. She worked for entertainment magazines and tabloids in New York and Los Angeles, including the *Hollywood Reporter.* Many aspiring young writers might think it was a dream job. Clare reported on the lives and travels of celebrities including Britney Spears, Brad Pitt, and Angelina Jolie. However, Clare eventually grew tired of this work and turned most of her attention to fantasy fiction writing.

She also worked part-time at a children's bookstore. There, her interest in the books she had read as a child was renewed.

So was her penchant for writing fiction. "I started writing [fiction] again," she recounts on her website, "and went through several novel ideas before I moved to New York City from Los Angeles."

On the *Cynsations* blog, Cynthia Leitich Smith asked Clare what she would tell herself if she could look back on her early fiction writing attempts. "Don't be so hard on yourself" was her immediate response. She explained, "I thought everything had to be perfect before I could show it to anyone, which means I never got any feedback on anything, and without feedback I couldn't work on improving . . . Eventually, I learned to share work with people even when it was in its rough stages without worrying that they'd be filled with scorn and hatred."

FOCUS ON FANTASY FICTION

While working as an entertainment journalist, at the suggestion of a friend she began writing fan fiction based on the phenomenally popular Harry Potter series. Her Draco Trilogy (*Draco Dormiens, Draco Sinister,* and *Draco Veritas*) has wizards Harry Potter and Draco Malfoy, his rival, accidentally switching bodies when a chemical experiment goes awry. She wrote other Harry Potter spin-offs as well as *The Very Secret Diaries*, spun from J. R. R. Tolkien's *The Lord of the Rings*.

A scene from the film set of *Harry Potter and the Order of the Phoenix*. In her early years as a fantasy writer, Clare wrote Harry Potter fan fiction.

Her fan fiction acquired a significant following, which helped her break into mainline fantasy fiction publishing. (She deleted her extensive fan fiction work from the Internet after selling rights to the Mortal Instruments.)

Clare's first fiction sale was "The Girl's Guide to Defeating the Dark Lord," a short story. It was published in 2004 as part of *Turn the Other Chick*, an anthology of humorous fantasy short stories and

READERS BECOME WRITERS: THE FAN FICTION PHENOMENON

Practically all professional writers have gotten their inspiration from reading. Most of them cite favorite authors as major influences on their work, with many fiction writers basing their characters on those of authors who preceded them. This method of developing new works of fiction has been practiced for centuries.

The World Wide Web has made instant, online publication possible for amateur writers. With it has come an explosion of fan fiction, where avid fans of best-selling books write their own stories and even novels about some of the characters they enjoy. They place the characters in plots of their own imagining, sometimes making villains of heroes and vice versa. Fan fiction is especially common in the genres of fantasy, horror, and mystery.

Fan fiction writers don't get paid for what they write, and their works can be accessed online free of charge. The best of them, though, develop followings of their own. Their popularity as fan fiction writers can showcase their writing talent and eventually lead to profitable book contracts. Such was the case with Cassandra Clare, who once wrote prolifically about characters in the Harry Potter and *Lord of the Rings* series.

The Internet today houses large groups of fan fiction enthusiasts and whole networks devoted to the efforts of fan writers. Some established authors oppose the trend, considering it a form of theft of their creativity and a violation of copyright law. Others—including Clare—encourage it. To them and their publishers, it's an excellent way to broaden the popularity of their original works, increasing rather than undermining their book sales.

Clare is also enthusiastic about fan art, amateur artwork by readers based on characters and scenes in their favorite authors' books. She has featured some of her own fans' illustrations on her website.

novellas penned by various authors. Since then, a number of her short stories have been published.

By 2004, Clare had begun working on *City of Bones*. It is the first of many novels that record the heroic battles and investigations of Shadowhunters, an angel-descended race of earthly protectors and peacekeepers. In 2006, she put all other work aside and turned her full energy and time to fantasy fiction. She says she has no regrets about abandoning the entertainment beat and, as she declares on her website, "hopes never to have to write about Paris Hilton again."

At that point, Clare was on the brink of achieving her breakthrough as a writer. Within two years, she would be a best-selling author. In the process, she would open a window for young readers into a surreal, exciting world invisible to the human eye: the realm of valiant Nephilim and the evil forces they encounter.

A MANUAL FOR SHADOWHUNTER FANS

Keeping details straight in the magic environs of Clare's best-selling series the Mortal Instruments and the Infernal Devices can be a challenge for new readers to the books and even established fans. With her husband Joshua Lewis, Clare has

Clare previews a scene during the filming of *The Mortal Instruments: City of Bones* with her husband, Joshua Lewis *(left),* and director Harald Zwart *(right).*

developed an informative and entertaining guide-book. *The Shadowhunter's Codex* (the *Codex*), an "illustrated guide to the knowledge and lore of the Shadowhunter world," was revised in October 2013. Clare describes the book as "part encyclopedia, part history, part training manual."

The *Codex* invites fans to join the Shadowhunters, or Nephilim. Readers are given the Shadowhunter oath and admonished to commit it to memory. "Joining the Nephilim," the *Codex* declares, "is not like becoming a mundane [human] policeman, or even a mundane soldier. 'Shadowhunter' is not what you do; it is who you are. Every aspect of your life will change to accommodate the holy assignment you have been chosen for."

Nephilim, as defined by the *Codex*, are "the appointed warriors on Earth of the Angel Raziel. We are appointed specifically to control and preside over the demonic in our world, both demons and the super-natural creatures born of their presence among us."

Raziel gave his Shadowhunters magic tools called "mortal instruments" with which to carry out their work a thousand years ago. He created Idris, a European country invisible to humans, where Nephilim can retreat and live away from demons as well as humans. He also gave them the "Gray Book," which enables them to use angel magic for protection. Little is known about the first ancient Nephilim, who Raziel named Jonathan Shadowhunter.

Besides Shadowhunters, the *Codex* defines demons—truly evil entities—as well as different types of "Downworlders," whose magic characteristics can be used for good. Downworlders include the following:

- Werewolves: Humans who can periodically turn into wolf-like creatures.
- Vampires: Attracted to human blood. (Though always treated as evil in traditional literature, some vampire characters in twenty-first-century fantasy fiction are good but tragic.)
- Warlocks: Traditionally considered male witches or magicians, although females are also among the warlocks in the writings of Clare and other modern authors.
- Faeries: Mischievous supernatural spirits.

In *Clockwork Angel*, the first volume of the Infernal Devices, one of the Shadowhunters explains to an initiate that the Nephilim are "a race, if you will, of people, people with special abilities. We are stronger and swifter than most humans. We are able to conceal ourselves with magics called glamours. And we are especially skilled at killing demons." A

Downworlder, she adds, is "a being—a *person*—who is part supernatural in origin. Vampires, werewolves, faeries, warlocks—they are all Downworlders."

Downworlders and Shadowhunters historically were enemies but, as a result of signed accords, exist in an uneasy alliance in Clare's fiction series.

Readers of the *Codex* are taught such things as the correct use of the vital "stele," a handheld magic weapon/tool, and armor. They learn how Shadowhunters kill demons and find descriptions of such strange items as the "pyxis." They are introduced to special beings such as Silent Brothers, Iron Sisters, and the Forsaken. Veteran Shadowhunters can "brush up on their demon languages."

The Shadowhunter's Codex is rich in humor. It includes "Discussion Questions and Things to Try" and appendices of Nephilim history. Illustrations include images of Idris, the mystic homeland of the Shadowhunters, and depictions of primary characters. Handwritten notes from some of them appear in the margins.

JUST FOR TEENS

In "Kids' Q&A" with Powell's Books, a major U.S. bookstore chain, Clare was asked why she chose to write books for young readers. "I write books for teenagers," she replied, "because when I was

Young fans of Clare's novels gave the movie version of *City of Bones* an enthusiastic reception when it was released in August 2013.

a teenager, that was the best reading time of my life. It was the time I experienced reading the most intensely and read the most widely and with the most excitement. I wanted a chance to experience that again through writing for teens."

While Clare was trying to sell *City of Bones*, one editor who looked at her proposal asked if she would consider reworking it as an adult novel revolving around adult main characters. She declined.

From the outset, she had envisioned teenaged characters, and she stuck with them.

When she began writing the book, she thought of
it simply as a romantic fantasy novel, not specifically
as a novel for young adult readers. "The characters
simply happened to be teenagers," she reflected in
answering a question posted at her website. She
played with the notion of making them adults, "but I
knew it wouldn't work. I wanted to tell a story about
characters at that crucial life stage just between
adolescence and adulthood, where your choices
determine the kind of person you're going to be
rather than reflect who you already are."

CREATING THE SHADOWHUNTERS

The landscape of Manhattan—which Clare says is her favorite metropolis in the world—was the underlying inspiration for the Mortal Instruments series. After she moved to New York, the epic series began to formulate in her mind. An important moment during the concept process was a visit to a friend's Greenwich Village tattoo shop. The tattoo artist showed her some age-old runes, strange patterns warriors wore for protection.

Although her books are classified as young adult fantasy or urban fantasy, Clare envisioned the Mortal Instruments series as "a romance with an action-adventure background." She already had in mind the romantic ingredients of the plot. The skin runes gave her the idea for a system of magic involving her central characters. In her forthcoming fantasy series, runes would become powerful devices used by her fictional race of demon slayers. (The author wears no tattoos herself. She quips that she is "not that cool.")

City of Bones, the first book in the series, took more than a year to complete, beginning in early 2004. She had drafted about ten chapters, constantly revising as she progressed, when a writer friend introduced her to a literary agent, Barry

Runes and other mysterious symbols are popular adornments of Clare's fans. Runes are sources of power for the heroines and heroes in Clare's novels.

Goldblatt. Goldblatt was impressed by what she had done. He suggested further revisions. They sold the project for $75,000 as a three-book series to Margaret K. McElderry Books, owned by major publisher Simon & Schuster. The sale was based on the still-incomplete first volume and in-depth outlines of the next two.

She had never attempted a novel like *City of Bones*, and she acknowledges it was a struggle. It literally underwent dozens of revisions. "I'd start a chapter, then go back and revise it, then write a little more, then go back and revise it from the beginning again," she recounted to Cynthia Leitich Smith on the *Cynsations* blog. "Essentially I was just rewriting the first chapter over and over, and never figuring out what happened next.

"Finally I decided to skip the beginning entirely and write through from Chapter Three, and for whatever reason that worked for me—I was able to work through building the [Shadowhunters'] world, and then go back later and establish that world more fully in the beginning, because now I really knew it."

A CAST OF CRYPTIC CHARACTERS

Clare's novels are particularly rich in characterization. Each individual is unique and fascinating.

The heroine of the series is Clary Fray, a teenager who is thrust into the domain of Shadowhunters and other supernatural races when her mother disappears. Physically, Clary is small, inexperienced at combat, and easily frightened, but she possesses a formidable inner toughness and determination. A gifted artist, she is intelligent and clever—but she has a knack for getting herself and her friends into trouble with impulsive reactions and unwise choices. In part, Clary mirrors one of the author's young friends who, like the fictitious leading character, is slight of build, but tough, and an artist.

Other main characters include the following:

- Simon Lewis. Clary's best friend is bookish, funny, and attentive to her well-being.

Clary Fray, a teen in turmoil, is the leading character in The Mortal Instruments series. She is portrayed in the movie by actress Lily Collins.

A wannabe garage band musician who can't dance, Simon appears in the original book as an ordinary mundane but later in the series is revealed to be a vampire. Clare says that from the inception of the Mortal Instruments, she intended for him to become a vampire, but she was saddened when the time came for his change from a human. As a result, however, he becomes a more prominent figure.

- Jace Lightwood. Clary is hopelessly attracted to the star Shadowhunter, who is startlingly handsome and athletic, and possesses a relentlessly sarcastic wit. A deepening affection grows between Clary and Jace until a stunning revelation near the end of *City of Bones* throws their relationship into utter confusion.
- Alec Lightwood. Alec is the young Shadowhunter paired with Jace as battle comrades. They are *parabatai*, pledged to fight together and look out for each other's safety, and are brothers by adoption. Clary learns that Alec is gay, but that is not a focal aspect of his character; foremost, he is a trained action hero like Jace. Clare says Jace has been readers' favorite character, although

judging from fan mail, Alec is almost as popular.

- Isabelle Lightwood. Alec's younger sister is a skilled Shadowhunter in her own right.
- Hodge Starkweather. The kindly tutor and leader of young Shadowhunters at their Institute in New York is not what he seems at first. Hodge is frequently accompanied by a clever raven named Hugin.
- Magnus Bane. The high warlock of Brooklyn has special powers and loves to throw parties for a variety of Downworld guests. Ageless, he figures prominently in the Mortal Instruments and the Infernal Devices, which is set more than a century earlier. Clare, who describes Magnus as a "trickster figure," was worried that his character would be cut from the film version of the book and was especially excited to see his onscreen portrayal.
- Luke Garroway. A lifelong friend and love interest of Clary's mother, Jocelyn, Luke is revealed to be a werewolf leader and ally of the Shadowhunters.
- Valentine Morgenstern. The ultimate nemesis who seeks to control and transform the Shadowhunters, Valentine turns out to have an astonishing connection to Clary.

New principal characters are introduced with subsequent books in the series.

A NEW BEST-SELLING AUTHOR

Initially, Clare intended for the Mortal Instruments to be a trilogy. *City of Bones* was published in 2007, followed by *City of Ashes* in 2008 and *City of Glass* in 2009. Completing *City of Glass* left her with mixed emotions. On one hand, she was relieved to be done with what had been a massive research and writing project. On the other, she felt depressed at the prospect of parting with her series' characters, to whom she'd developed a deep author's attachment.

Happily for her—and even more so for her fans—the Mortal Instruments continued with a sequel trilogy. *City of Fallen Angels* was published in 2011 followed by *City of Lost Souls* in 2012. The series finally concluded in May 2014, with publication of the sixth volume, *City of Heavenly Fire.*

City of Bones quickly became a best seller. Sales no doubt were boosted by the alluring cover image of a long-curled, shirtless young Shadowhunter, his chest and biceps covered with mysterious tattoos. The entire series got an important marketing lift in the form of praise from Stephenie Meyer, best-selling author of the vampire romance novel *Twilight* and its three sequels. A quote of recommendation by Meyer appears on the cover of each book in the Mortal Instruments.

City of Bones became enormously popular within months of publication. Subsequent Clare novels have joined it on various best-seller lists.

Meyer wrote, "The Mortal Instruments series is a story world that I *love* to live in. Beautiful." *Publishers Weekly* praised the setting of *City of Bones* as "spot-on, informed equally by neo-gothic horror films and . . . modern fantasy leanings . . . Werewolves, vampires, angels and fairies all fit in this ambitious milieu. At the core, though, this is a compelling story about family secrets and coming-of-age identity crises." *Kirkus Reviews* called *City of Bones* "lush and fun." From *Entertainment Weekly*: "Prepare to be hooked."

A review in *School Library Journal* predicted that "this version of New York, full of Buffyesque teens who are trying to save the world, is entertaining and will have fantasy readers anxiously awaiting the next book in the series." However, it judged, "The characters are sporadically characterized and tend toward behavior that is both predictable and slightly repellent—Clary finds out who her real father is about 200 pages after readers will have figured it out."

The book won more than a dozen special and regional book awards. Among the honors was a 2008 American Library Association Teens Top Ten Award. Eventually, the series was translated into more than thirty languages.

Clare insists that none of her fiction writing is autobiographical, despite the similarity in

CASSANDRA CLARE: FILM CONSULTANT

Many critics believe by and large that a film is never as good as the book on which it's based. When asked if she's uneasy about the prospect of her novels being made into movies, Clare expresses the practical view. She explains on her website, "If you don't risk having a bad movie made out of your book, you'll never get a good movie made out of your book, either."

The movie *Mortal Instruments: City of Bones* was released in 2013. Clare was invited to participate in the casting process, during which various actors' audition tapes were discussed. During filming, director Harald Zwart woke her up with a late-night phone call for advice on one of the scene takes.

After an early screening of *Mortal Instruments: City of Bones*, longtime fans expressed to Clare their excited approval. "The fact that they loved it was the thing that meant the most to me," she told the *Hollywood Reporter*'s Sophie Schillaci.

But the film met with mostly negative to lukewarm reviews and was not a notable box office success. Generally, critics felt it offered little to make it stand out in its movie genre. A spokesman for the production company acknowledged to the press that the film "obviously underperformed." Clare's fans were enthusiastic, however, and the film sequel, *Mortal Instruments: City of Ashes*, was tentatively scheduled to begin production in 2014.

names between Clary, the heroine of the Mortal Instruments, and her own last name (or the fact that they are both redheads). She does endeavor, though, to imagine herself in the shoes of the individuals she is writing about. Failure to accomplish that, she believes, would leave the author uninspired and readers bored.

Some of the minor characters, such as Simon's friends in the Mortal Instruments, are based on

Many of the places referred to in Clare's series are real. Among them is the Renwick Smallpox Hospital, now a formidable ruin on Roosevelt Island in Manhattan.

personal friends of Clare's. Also, she draws certain traits of her fictional characters from people she knows—Clary's artistic talent, for example, and Simon's unique style of humor.

Many of the geographical locations are real, although not all of those in the Mortal Instruments exist in Manhattan. Real-life sites include the Pandemonium Club, Dumont Hotel, Renwick Smallpox Hospital, Marble Cemetery, Taki's, Garroway's Books, and even the Institute. Isis, the Shadowhunters' homeland, is completely imaginary.

CHAPTER FOUR

TIME TRAVELING TO VICTORIAN LONDON

P ractically from the outset of her Shadowhunter concept, Clare realized the geographic range would probably be expanded. After all, she was creating a global organization of demon fighters. It only made sense to follow their adventures overseas. The next phase would step back in time to the 1870s and steam across the Atlantic to England to present the Infernal Devices, a prequel series to the Mortal Instruments.

The reason she based the new series in London was simple: London is among her very favorite cities. Her personal library has a large section of books from the English Victorian era, books she's been reading since childhood. She considers that period to be a turning point in history. Its frenzy of inventions gave people cause to believe ships really would be able to fly, perhaps in their lifetimes. Her Nephilim warriors were steeped in ancient fighting tactics and weaponry. How, she wondered, might they cope with new threats of evil that employed scary machines and technology?

QUOTES FROM THE PAST

Clare is a collector of quotations. In her extensive reading, she jots down passages and phrases that to her seem worth remembering. Eventually, some of them turn up in her writings.

Not surprisingly, quotes from the works of vintage English writers appear at chapter beginnings throughout the Infernal Devices. They include lines of poetry and statements from the pens of Lord Byron, Robert Browning, Alfred Tennyson, John Keats, William Shakespeare, and many others. Some of the authors were active during the 1870s, when her series is set. Others lived generations before that time. Their writings would have been familiar to readers of the day.

The Infernal Devices is "a little more Gothic and romantic than *Mortal Instruments*," she described in an interview with Cheryl Brody, "and a little less urban and punk, but it's still about a smart, tough heroine."

That heroine is Tessa Gray, an American orphan girl who journeys to London from New York to unite with her older brother—and is immediately thrown into the supernatural world Clare had created in her first series. As in the Mortal Instruments, Clare intertwines a complex theme of love with a central plot filled with page-turning action. Tessa's heart is torn between the two Nephilim who protect her, Will and Jem, best friends who are pledged to defend each other to the death.

A HISTORIC BRIDGE STIRS THE IMAGINATION

Just as exploring Manhattan with its fascinating sights, sounds, and people set the scene in her mind and shaped the plots for the Mortal Instruments, reconnoitering London did the same for the Infernal Devices. Clare was on the historic Blackfriars Bridge crossing the River

When Clare crossed the famous Blackfriars Bridge in London, it gave her the idea for an action scene in *Clockwork Angel*, a new novel then in development.

Thames when she suddenly envisioned the bridge on a murky night. A boy and girl stood at the rail staring out over the riverfront, unaware an "army of clock-work creatures" was approaching them from one end, she explained in "Author Interview: Cassandra Clare" on the *Bookish Type* blog. It spurred the plot taking shape in her imagination and would result in a dramatic scene in *Clockwork Angel.*

Inexplicably, the young couple wore Victorian attire. Clare was "surprised to realize that the story was going to be historical," she explained on the *Bookish Type.* "I tried to update it, but it just wouldn't budge—as the characters and the tale grew, I knew these people were the ancestors of the characters in the TMI [The Mortal Instruments] books and that their story would contain elements that would enhance and explain later events."

The author had a bit of difficulty convincing her publisher that the Victorian London backdrop could appeal to young fantasy fiction fans. She pointed out similar teen or crossover novels that had achieved sales success.

Drawing on her extensive personal knowledge of London, Clare strove to depict England's capital as it existed historically. She went to great lengths to present an accurate setting. While developing the Infernal Devices, she devoted six months of her reading time exclusively to material pertaining to the

Victorian era. This included books, travelers' journals, and newspaper articles published in the nineteenth century. She revisited London during her research, took countless photographs, and used city maps of the 1880s to chart the routes her characters would take from place to place, describing landmarks and streets along the way. She hired an assistant to locate obscure images of some of the sites.

Clare did not confine her reading and research to England. She also studied the period history, literature, and geography of France, China, and the United States because segments of the plot take place in Paris, New York, and Shanghai. Although the cityscapes have changed a lot over time, she wanted to be sure readers are oriented correctly to where landmarks were situated in relation to one another.

In "A Note on Tessa's London" at the conclusion of *Clockwork Angel*, Clare explains that her description of the city in the nineteenth century is "an admixture of the real and the unreal, the famous and the forgotten. The geography of real Victorian London is preserved as much as possible, but there were times that wasn't possible." Real-life settings include Hampstead Heath, Hyde Park, the Strand, Blackfriars Bridge, and Carlton Square.

Clare also had to take care in wording the text for the series. She knew she could not afford to bore young readers with stilted dialogue and terminology of the period and place. At the same time, for the sake of historic accuracy, she could not use teen talk that has become common only in recent decades. "Teens would not really be enthused with my attempt to replicate slang in a quaint style of dialogue," she explained in a Metro.us blog interview, "Putting the Hard Sell on Steampunk." "I went with not using any anachronistic terms . . . or phraseologies or idioms that would not have existed, but keeping the characters' speech simple and straightforward."

Still, to maintain an authentic feel, she peppered the narratives with some antiquated terminology of the times. "Penny dreadfuls" referred to novels sensational for their violence. City streets were illuminated at night by gas lamps in the years before electric power. People who needed to travel more than a few blocks went from place to place in hansom cabs, which

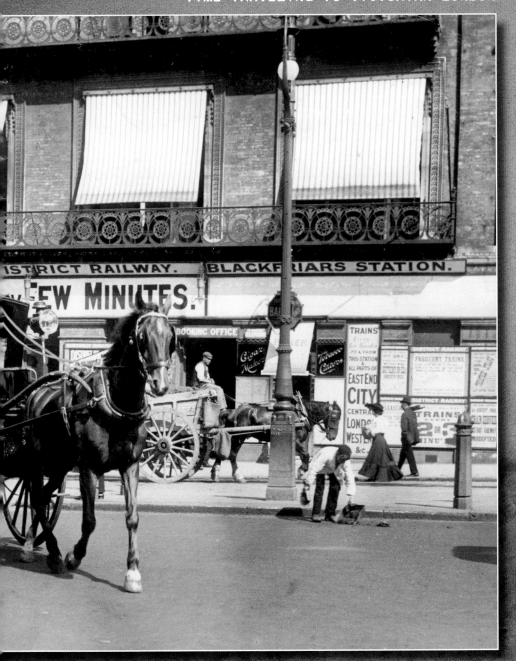

During the years before motorized taxis, London's citizens got around in two-wheel, horse-drawn hansom cabs. In The Infernal Devices, Clare alludes to many such features common to that era.

were two-wheel, single-horse carriages in which the driver sat on an elevated rear perch on the outside. Clare mentions street peddlers hawking hokey-pokey (ice cream) lumps.

SEQUELS, PREQUELS, AND OTHER SPECIAL CHALLENGES

Clare's overall plotting plan for the Infernal Devices series is different from that of the Mortal Instruments. *City of Bones*, the opening volume in the latter series, has a pleasing, definite conclusion—even though it ends with many unanswered questions. Readers are left wondering what adventures and mysteries might engage the main characters in the future and whether there will be a sequel. Even if there was no sequel, *City of Bones* finishes on a note of satisfactory closure.

Clockwork Angel, by contrast, leaves major threads of the plot unresolved. The main villain has escaped and vows revenge on the Shadowhunters. One of the heroes is in an emotionally painful quandary. The situation at the end demands further development.

Clare says authors of series must be very careful in developing sequels and prequels. If a series of original books has an established base of fans, roughly half of them, she's discovered, fear the forthcoming series will cover no fresh ground. The rest will worry that it will be starkly different, giving them too few threads to connect with the original plot and characters. Authors, she concludes, can't solve that dilemma and should not try. They simply should tell a new story the way it comes to them and leave the judgment to the fans.

A NEW CHAMPION: TESSA GRAY, WARLOCK

As in the Mortal Instruments, the central character of the Infernal Devices is a girl suddenly caught up in an underworld of magic. Tessa Gray is captured by devious forces immediately upon her arrival in London—forces that seem to know things about her that she does not realize herself. Tessa discovers she is a warlock endowed with the rare ability (even for warlocks) to change into the personage of someone else.

Other primary characters in *Clockwork Angel* include the following:

- The Dark Sisters. Confined inside what would come to be called the "Dark House," Tessa is forcibly trained over a period of weeks to refine her power by Mrs. Dark, a demon, and Mrs. Black, a warlock. They disclose that they are making her ready for marriage to the Magister.

- Will Herondale. Tessa immediately feels an attraction to Will, the striking young Shadowhunter who rescues her from the Dark House. He takes her to safety inside the Institute for Shadowhunters in London.
- Jem Carstairs. Though pale (suffering from a strange addictive disorder) and gentle in nature, Will's parabatai Jem is an able fighter. Jem and Tessa also forge a close relationship, which becomes a source of romantic tension.
- Jessamine Lovelace. Orphan child of Shadowhunter parents, Jessamine is housed in the Institute. She hates the Nephilim life and plots to escape into the real world—perhaps with Tessa's help—but is hampered by unforeseen circumstances.
- Charlotte and Henry Branwell. The Branwells, heads of the Institute in London, are Shadowhunters themselves. Although just in her twenties, Charlotte is much like a mother figure. Her husband is constantly in the basement experimenting with weapons and tools (infernal devices), which often malfunction when taken into action.

- Nathaniel Gray. Nate is the older brother Tessa has come to London to find. The book's plot turns on deception upon deception, and Nate proves to be part of it.
- The Magister. The Magister is the leader of forces bent on destroying the Nephilim forever. To accomplish his obsession, he must make Tessa his wife because of her special power. His character is perhaps the most intriguing in *Clockwork Angel* because the reader is kept guessing as to the Magister's true identity.

As in the Mortal Instruments, the central characters—the Shadowhunters based at the Institute—are part of a great municipal network of Nephilim. In the Mortal Instruments, the New York organization is called the Conclave. In the Infernal Devices, the Nephilim are called the Enclave. They all have the same mandate: to protect humans and maintain peace and order in the underworld.

ANOTHER IMMEDIATE BEST SELLER

The Infernal Devices series entered publication while the Immortal Instruments, her longer original series, was still in progress. Volume One, *Clockwork Angel*, came out in 2010. It was followed by *Clockwork Prince* in 2011 and *Clockwork Princess* in 2013.

School Library Journal said of *Clockwork Angel*, "The action-heavy plot takes off from the first page, propelling readers toward a dramatic conclusion." From a *Booklist* review: "Packed with battles, romantic entanglements, and tantalizing foreshadowing, this will have readers clamoring for the next installment." *Publishers Weekly* reported, "The events often read as bleakly as the Victorian London weather, punctuated by Clare's trademark humor, empathy, and authentic characters, who fight their own flaws and tragic pasts as often as they do evil. Mysteries, misdirection, and riddles abound, and while there are some gruesome moments, they never feel gratuitous. Fans of the Mortal Instruments series and newcomers alike won't be disappointed."

Like *City of Bones* in the Mortal Instruments series, *Clockwork Angel* made prominent best-seller lists, including those of the *New York Times*, the *Los Angeles Times*, the *Wall Street Journal*, *USA Today*, and the *Globe and Mail* in Toronto. It made the "Indigo Books Top 10 of 2010" in the teen fiction category.

ON TYPING, TUNES, AND MORE: CASSANDRA CLARE AT WORK

C lare does most of her writing away from home to avoid the distractions of her cats and routine interruptions. So she is often seen writing in restaurants and coffee shops. She finds it helpful to work with friends around. They help keep her disciplined, she says, which is especially important when on deadline.

When she does work at home, it usually is in her tiny office. Besides her computer and an ample supply of books within arm's reach, she pins on a wall some of the letters and art sent by fans. Clare finds them a source of encouragement.

Probably the most surprising detail about her writing style is that she is a two-fingered typist. Any writer can attest that's a remarkable feat, considering the

CHAPTER FIVE

enormous extent of her text in print—not to mention the draft passages that were discarded during multiple editing stages.

She constantly has music playing in the background while writing. Clare has assembled certain playlists to listen to while writing about different characters and settings. This, she says, puts her in the appropriate frame of mind. Visitors to her website can find playlists of the songs she listened to while working on *City of Bones*—including Neko Case, OK Go, the Decemberists, and Death Cab for Cutie—and *Clockwork Angel*—such as Keane, Tegan and Sara, the Flaming Lips, and Secret Machines.

IT ALL BEGINS WITH OUTLINES

For Clare, crafting a series of best-selling fiction novels begins with a preconceived master plot. Before she sits down to write, she knows essentially where her book or series will take the reader.

"The plots of both the Mortal Instruments series and the Infernal Devices series," she elaborates at her website, "rest on a lot of carefully planned misdirection and foreshadowing—both of which are very difficult to do if you don't really know where you're going."

Clare typically works on her fantasy novels while listening to music and posts playlists on her website. Among her favorite musicians is singer-songwriter Neko Case.

Structure, for her, is important: "Some people sit down and just wing it; I can't do that." Structure involves foreknowledge of "not only what's going to happen, but when it needs to happen, when clues need to be dropped, and where and when certain things need to be emphasized or de-emphasized."

To accomplish that, she outlines meticulously. She outlines the overall series, each book within it, and the sequence of scenes in each chapter. "I

"INSPIRATION MUST FIND YOU WORKING"

Many fans have wondered what inspires Cassandra Clare to write and what keeps her motivated for months and even years to see a book through to completion. Her view of "inspiration" is completely practical. Everyone has frequent moments of inspiration, she believes. They can come from books, films, songs, artworks, beautiful scenes, or any number of other triggers. But most are fleeting and quickly forgotten.

"Inspiration has to be noted," she says on her website, "then expanded on and shaped and turned into something interesting or important through lots of hard work—developing a learned set of skills, and applying them, and not expecting it to be easy."

The real issue, she adds, is determination. "Some things take hard work and determination to complete; novels are one of those things. Learning to force yourself to work on your writing is not appreciably different from learning to force yourself to do anything else," she says.

She cites a quotation from painter Pablo Picasso: "Inspiration does exist, but it must find you working." A big part of the challenge for every writer, she believes, is learning to take advantage of inspirations when they come.

also outline each character's arc—where they start out, what they want when they start out, where their chief moments of growth/discovery are, and how they end up," she says

The course of the story may change as she writes. When that happens, she tweaks her outline to accommodate the changes, and then proceeds.

On the "Writing Advice" page of her site (http://www.cassandraclare.com/writing-advice), Clare points aspiring young authors to resources about outlining, dealing with writer's block, the publishing process, and other writing aids.

CHARACTERIZATION, ACTION, HUMOR

Clary Fray and Tessa Gray, the respective protagonists of the Mortal Instruments and the Infernal Devices, are strong central figures who draw readers from one novel to the next. But Clare is noted for her skill at creating not only heroines but entire casts of interesting individuals. Some are based in part on people she knows. Some are completely imagined. "Creating characters," she said in an interview with Cheryl Brody, "is like throwing together ingredients for a recipe. I take characteristics I like and dislike in real people I know, or know of, and use them to embellish and define characters."

Cast of complex characters *(left to right)*: Clary Fray (played by Lily Collins),
Simon Lewis (Robert Sheehan), Jace Wayland (Jamie Campbell Bower),
Alexander Lightwood (Kevin Zegers), and Isabelle Lightwood (Jemima West).

The ability of crafty characterization is but one of Clare's writing fortes. Fluid movement from scene to scene keeps the reader engaged from start to finish—and her action sequences are guaranteed page-turners.

Creating fight scenes is one of the most difficult aspects of writing for Clare, but one she particularly enjoys. While developing *City of Bones*, she conferred with a theatrical coordinator of action scenes. When things are happening very quickly, each moment must be kept in accurate context—for example, remembering where each participant is positioned, relative to everyone else. She prefers to write fight scenes when a friend is present. They literally act out a scene to make sure the movements she describes could really work.

In an interview with Metro.us, "Putting the Hard Sell on Steampunk," she revealed, "More than once I've been at my friend Holly's house and we act out a fight scene and her husband comes home and says, 'I don't even want to know why you're fighting each other in the living room.'"

Although the underlying tone of her two best-selling series is dark, Clare provides healthy doses of comic relief in frequent quips by some of her characters, most notably Jace in the Mortal Instruments. Readers find them especially delightful when they're injected into unlikely scenes. Clare recognizes the tremendous value of humor and knows how to covey it, but she finds it difficult to explain to aspiring young writers where it comes from. She considers herself intrinsically sarcastic, and many of her friends are naturally funny: "I keep my ears out for funny conversations my friends have and often adapt aspects of them for my books. If you really want to learn how to write humor, there are books out there about it, although I tend to think either you have an ear for what's funny—which is generally about timing and word choice—or you don't."

Clare says the final book in a series, for her, is particularly difficult. In an interview with Donna Freitas of *Publishers Weekly*, she explained, "The more questions you pose, the more work you have to do to finish things up . . . People warned me that the last book would be the most difficult because you are stringing readers along with a lot of promises. But then, when you actually get to answer the promises, it's very satisfying."

WRITING AND PUBLISHING IN THE INTERNET AGE

The Internet has changed practically everything about the book industry, from research and writing to marketing and publicity. Clare says social networking and keeping her website updated are vital. Teenagers in particular, she observes, get most of their information about books and authors online, including book signing schedules and news about works in progress, publishing dates, and film projects. The Internet also gives readers an opportunity to interact with their favorite authors, submitting fan mail and keeping current with blog posts and Twitter tweets. She laments that the advantages of electronic communication were not available to her when she was a child immersed in books.

Clare continues to read voraciously, as she has since childhood. Her home is filled with books— "getting underfoot, stacking up in piles," she muses to her website visitors. She posts a list of suggested books for young adult readers. Among the

Clare's favorite authors include Stephenie Meyer, famous for her vampire romance series Twilight. Meyer's endorsement helped promote The Mortal Instruments novels.

numerous authors whose works she recommends are Kelley Armstrong, Robin McKinley, Stephenie Meyer, Suzanne Collins, Lauren Myracle, Holly Black, Scott Westerfeld, and Laini Taylor.

In advising young writers, she tells them to recruit the help of a personal evaluator, someone whose opinion they value and whom they can trust to read their work and offer objective, constructive comments. "Even the most skilled writers aren't the best judges of their own work," she pointed out in the *Seventeen* magazine interview with Cheryl Brody, "so having someone else look at it and give you feedback is invaluable."

Above all, she says, they should write about what's dear to their hearts. For example, if they most enjoy being funny, they shouldn't force themselves to write about serious topics. "You're a reader as well as a writer, so write what you'd want to read," she says.

CASSANDRA CLARE TODAY

Cassandra Clare and her husband, Josh Lewis, live in Amherst, Massachusetts, with several pet cats they've rescued. Music is a constant in Clare's life, even while writing. She enjoys different musical genres.

Aside from reading and writing, travel is her dearest interest. She is on the go frequently and has done some of her writing in foreign locations. In "Kids' Q&A," an interview for Powell's Books, Clare said that her greatest thrill is "being on a plane or train headed for some fabulous and exciting destination I've never visited before." She's been teased that if it weren't for family and career ties, she probably would have no permanent home—and she agrees.

Her favorite holiday is Chanukah. "Almost all Jewish holidays center around food, but Chanukah has the best food with the potato latkes and the chocolate gelt," she said in the Powell's Books interview. "Also with dreydl playing you have religiously sanctioned gambling which allows you to take your parents' money away."

Chocolate coins (gelt), favorites of generations of candy lovers, appeal to Clare. Her favorite holiday is Chanukah, mainly because of its culinary enticements.

RECENT AND FUTURE WRITING PROJECTS

After completing *City of Heavenly Fire*, the last novel in the Mortal Instruments series, Clare collaborated with authors Sarah Rees Brennan and Maureen Johnson in the Bane Chronicles, a series of short stories about her recurring character Magnus Bane. Brennan is an Irish writer whose first young adult fantasy series of novels, the Demon's Lexicon trilogy, began publication in 2009; a follow-up series is the Lynburn Legacy. Johnson is an American author of young adult fiction noted for several well-received novel series including Suite Scarlett and Shades of London.

Tales in the Bane Chronicles series, which is published by Simon & Schuster, began with "What Really Happened in Peru," released in April 2013. They initially were produced as e-books and audiobooks, with professional actors doing the narration. The collection was combined in a print edition that appeared in September 2014. The Bane Chronicles quickly joined the *New York Times* children's best-seller list.

The Magisterium series, cowritten with Holly Black, is for a slightly younger reading audience than her first two series. Black became widely known for the Spiderwick Chronicles, a series of eleven children's fantasy books (2003–2009). Clare and Black are longtime friends who frequently share writing ideas. Certain characters in Clare's novels sometimes appear in books by Black, and vice versa.

The first book in the Magisterium series, *The Iron Trial*, was published in September 2014 by Scholastic Books. The five-book series will chronicle events in the life of central character Callum Hunt between the ages of twelve and seventeen, after he becomes embroiled in the world of magic.

Meanwhile, Clare has begun writing a three-book companion series to the Mortal Instruments, this one set in Los Angeles several years after the conclusion of the New York adventures with *City of Heavenly Fire.* The Dark Artifices series involves a new set of young demon fighters based in the Institute at LA. Protagonist Shadowhunters are Emma Carstairs and Julian Blackthorn. *Lady Midnight*, the first volume of the Dark Artifices, is scheduled for publication in 2015. Planned sequels will be *The Prince of Shadows* and *The Queen of Air and Darkness*. Few details are available at this writing, but on her website Clare promises "love, magic, romantic confusion, etc." and adds that "it is reasonable to assume

CRINGING AT CARNAGE

Much of the action in Cassandra Clare's novels involves fight scenes with bloody slashing and stabbing, as well as plenty of severed limbs. Ironically, the author confesses, she cringes at the thought of bloodletting.

While living in London as a child, she became enthralled by the Sherlock Holmes stories. One of them, however, disturbed her a great deal. In the story "The Engineer's Thumb," a young mechanical engineer loses a thumb while escaping through a window from the site of a counterfeiting operation. Clare lay awake at night for a week after reading the tale.

In an interview for the *Persnickety Snark* blog, Adele Walsh asked Clare which of the character types in her books are more like her: Shadowhunter, vampire, or werewolf. "Shadowhunter," she answered without hesitation. "I'm actually really grossed out by blood and I think the turning into a werewolf thing would grate on me after a while."

that surviving characters from TMI [The Mortal Instruments] will make cameos. They will be in their early twenties so you'll get to see what they're up to in their more adult lives."

Early in 2014, yet another new series was announced. Walker Books bought United Kingdom, Australian, New Zealand, and export rights for a trilogy titled the Last Hours, a sequel to the Infernal Devices set twenty years afterward. The novels—*Chain of Thorns*, *Chain of Gold*, and *Chain of Iron*—are scheduled to begin publication in 2017.

As for films, *Mortal Instruments: City of Ashes* went into production in late 2013, soon after the release of *Mortal Instruments: City of Bones*. Production was halted, however, when the production company decided to rework the script. The status of the project was unknown at this writing. Clare points out that she has no control over the process, having sold the film rights.

Her works also are being developed as graphic novels with comic-style illustrations.

ENTERTAINMENT AND INSPIRATION

Asked what she hopes her readers will derive from her books, Clare says in the end, she simply wants them to have a wonderful reading experience. But she notes that young readers likely pick up on certain themes, such as loyalty, love, and coming of age. In the interview for *Persnickety*

Readers find Jace Wayland, portrayed by actor Jamie Campbell Bower, the most popular character in The Mortal Instruments series. Jace is noted for his handsome features and sarcastic wit.

Snark, she explained to Adele Walsh that the Mortal Instruments in part is "about family and what it means, and about making choices about who you are and who you want to be."

She hopes her leading characters might inspire others. Clary Fray, for instance, is far from perfect. Poor decisions combined with dangerous circumstances get her into precarious situations, and she feels terrified. But she somehow finds reserves of strength and courage to see her through. Hopefully, readers will relate, realizing they, like Clary, can stand up for their convictions even though they're imperfect and sometimes afraid.

Clare's books have different publishers in different international editions. Her publisher in the United States is Simon & Schuster. Russell Galen of Scovil Galen Ghosh is her literary agent, while her film associations are represented by the Gotham Group.

FAVORITES IN HER FICTION

Clare, who often signs her e-memos and blog posts "Cassie," says she has no favorite character in any of her writings, but she does relate more to certain individuals than others. She remarks that Simon in the Mortal Instruments and Tessa in the Infernal Devices have her traits of shyness and bookishness. Clare repeatedly singles out Simon,

MODEL MUSES

When asked which authors have been her greatest inspirations, Clare says there are too many to count. Different writers have impressed her with different aspects of their work. For example, she cites the attention to periodic detail that's obvious in the books of Dorothy Dunnett, a Scottish historical novelist best remembered for her six-volume series the Lymond Chronicles and its prequel series the House of Niccolò. She admires the humor P. G. Wodehouse injected into his novels, stories, poems, and plays. Among contemporary fantasy writers, she is intrigued by the way Philip Pullman is able to process complex issues, even for juvenile readers.

Clare considers J. K. Rowling, mastermind of the Harry Potter books, to be an author on a level all to herself. In "Author Interview: Cassandra Clare" on the *Bookish Type* blog, she noted Rowling's "ability to build a world within a world that feels real." To *Fortune* magazine's David Kaplan she summarized, "Nobody sells books like J.K. Rowling. We have a rule in publishing: Never compare anything to Harry Potter because it's like lightning in a bottle."

She believes the Twilight series of vampire romance books by Stephenie Meyer was pivotal in making novels written for young adults popular with older readers. "'Twilight' has an adult-friendly cover, and it has the beautiful, simple design that no one would feel embarrassed to carry around," she said in an interview for Metro.us, "Putting the Hard Sell on Steampunk." "It knocked down the barriers between the young adult sections and the rest of the store."

Clary Fray's best friend, as having a personality most like hers. Also, even though he eventually becomes a vampire, he is introduced in *City of Bones* as a normal human being—a true mundane—and thus serves as an important bridge for readers into the supernatural world Clare has created.

She has pointed to Sherlock Holmes as probably her all-time favorite character in fiction. And reading the Holmes books and stories, she says, helped her immensely in establishing a style of dialogue for her Victorian characters in the Infernal Devices that modern teen readers find easy to understand. Although Arthur Conan Doyle wrote most of the Holmes books and stories more than a century ago,

With multiple future projects scheduled, Clare is very busy. She divides her time between writing and attending book signings and other promotional events.

his writing is not as musty in tone as some of the other works of that period.

Clare's success began with her fan fiction writings based on Harry Potter and *The Lord of the Rings.* Now, a new wave of fan fiction writers are developing stories using her characters. Clare is not at all offended. "I totally support their writing of it," she told Alexandra Alter of the *Wall Street Journal.* "It's a huge compliment."

ON CASSANDRA CLARE

Birth date: July 27, 1973

Birthplace: Tehran, Iran

Current residence: Amherst, Massachusetts

Marital status: Married, to Josh Lewis

High school: Los Angeles, California

College: Clare majored in English and took some writing classes, but she described most of her writing training as "personal . . . totally irrelevant to my books."

Favorite authors: Dorothy Dunnett, P. G. Wodehouse, Arthur Conan Doyle, Philip Pullman, Stephenie Meyer, Kelley Armstrong, Suzanne Collins, J. K. Rowling, Holly Black, Robin McKinley, Scott Westerfeld, Laini Taylor, and Lauren Myracle

Favorite book as a teen: *Flowers in the Attic* by V. C. Andrews (but now she thinks it's a terrible book)

Interests: Traveling, reading

Previous occupation: Journalism, children's book-store staff worker

Favorite kind of cookie: Snickerdoodles

ON CASSANDRA CLARE'S WORK

The Mortal Instruments

City of Bones. New York, NY: Simon & Schuster, 2007.

Synopsis: Clary Fray, fifteen, and her best friend, Simon Lewis, go to a New York City dance club and find themselves drawn into a supernatural realm of demons, demon hunters (Shadowhunters), werewolves, warlocks, and other races. *City of Bones* is the first of six novels in The Mortal Instruments series following the adventures and intrigues of Clary, her friends and allies, and a frightful assortment of antagonists. A film based on the novel was released in 2013.

Honors: *New York Times* best seller; American Library Association Teens Top Ten Award (2008); Locus Award for Best First Novel, finalist (2007); Texas TAYSHAS title (2010); Abraham Lincoln High School Book Award (2010); Pacific Northwest Library Association Young Reader's Choice Award (2010).

City of Ashes. New York, NY: Simon & Schuster, 2008.

Honors: *New York Times* best seller; *USA Today* best seller; American Library Association Teens Top Ten Award (2009); International Reading Association Young Adults Choice Title (2010).

City of Glass. New York, NY: Simon & Schuster, 2009.

Honors: *New York Times* best seller; *USA Today* best seller; *Wall Street Journal* best seller; *Publishers Weekly* best seller; Indie Bound best seller; Children's Book Council Teen Choice Book of the Year, finalist (2010); American Library Association Teens Top Ten Award (2010).

City of Fallen Angels. New York, NY: Simon & Schuster, 2011.

Honors: *New York Times* best seller; *USA Today* best seller; *Wall Street Journal* best seller; *Publishers Weekly* best seller; Book-seller best seller; Barnes and Noble Best Book (2011); number one best seller in Australia and New Zealand.

City of Lost Souls. New York, NY: Simon & Schuster, 2012.

City of Heavenly Fire. New York, NY: Simon & Schuster, 2014.

The Infernal Devices

Clockwork Angel. New York, NY: Simon & Schuster, 2010.

Synopsis: Tessa Gray, a teenage orphan, journeys from New York by ship to England to reunite with her brother in 1878. She is immediately captured by supernatural forces for the purpose of exploiting an incredible power she is unaware she possesses. *Clockwork Angel* is the first of three novels in The Infernal Devices series. They are prequels to Clare's first best selling series, The Mortal Instruments.

Honors: *New York Times* best seller; *Globe and Mail* best seller; *Wall Street Journal* best-seller; *Los Angeles Times* best seller; *Publishers Weekly* best seller; *USA Today* best seller; Indie Bound best seller; New Atlantic Independent Booksellers Association best seller; Southern Indie Bookseller List best seller; YALSA Teens Top Ten Award (2011); Silver Inky Award (2011); Rita Award, finalist (2011); Indigo Books Top 10: Teen Fiction (2010); Barnes and Noble Top Ten Teen Books (2010); *Kansas City Star's* Top 100 Books of 2010; *VOYA* Perfect Ten.

Clockwork Prince. New York, NY: Simon & Schuster, 2011.

Honors: *New York Times* best seller; *Wall Street Journal* best seller; *USA Today* best seller; Los Angeles Library Best of 2011 Young Adult Book; Children's Book Council Teen Book of the Year (2012).

Clockwork Princess. New York, NY: Simon & Schuster, 2013.

The Bane Chronicles
"*What Really Happened in Peru.*" New York, NY: Simon & Schuster, 2013.

Synopsis: This begins a series of stories or novellas based on the character of warlock Magnus Bane, a central figure in The Mortal Instruments and The Infernal Devices series. They were written in collaboration with Sarah Rees Brennan and Maureen Johnson.

"*The Runaway Queen.*" New York, NY: Simon & Schuster, 2013.

"*Vampires, Scones, and Edmund Herondale.*" New York, NY: Simon & Schuster, 2013.

"*The Midnight Heir.*" New York, NY: Simon & Schuster, 2013.

"*The Rise of the Hotel Dumort.*" New York, NY: Simon & Schuster, 2013.

"*Saving Raphael Santiago.*" New York, NY: Simon & Schuster, 2013.

"*The Fall of the Hotel Dumort.*" New York, NY: Simon & Schuster, 2013.

"*What to Buy the Shadowhunter Who Has Everything (And Who You're Not Officially Dating Anyway).*" New York, NY: Simon & Schuster, 2013.

"The Last Stand of the New York Institute." New York, NY: Simon & Schuster, 2013.

"*The Course of True Love (and First Dates).*" New York, NY: Simon & Schuster, 2014.

Magisterium

The Iron Trial. New York, NY: Scholastic Press, 2014.

Synopsis: Cowritten with Holly Black, this begins a five-part series of fantasy novels following the adventures of teenager Callum Hunt. Subsequent books to be announced.

The Dark Artifices

Lady Midnight. 2015.

Synopsis: This begins a three-part series of novels featuring Emma Carstairs, a young Shadowhunter living in Los Angeles.

The Prince of Shadows. Publication date to be announced.

The Queen of Air and Darkness. Publication date to be announced.

The Last Hours

Synopsis: This sequel trilogy to The Infernal Devices is scheduled for publication in 2017.

The Mortal Instruments

"Clare's atmospheric setting is spot-on, informed equally by neo-gothic horror films and the modern fantasy leanings of Neil Gaiman. Werewolves, vampires, angels and fairies all fit in this ambitious milieu. At the core, though, this is a compelling story about family secrets and coming-of-age identity crises. Fans of the smart/chic horror typified by Buffy the Vampire Slayer will instantly fall for this new series." —*Publishers Weekly*

"The story's sensual flavor comes from the wealth of detail: demons with facial piercings, diners serving locusts and honey, pretty gay warlocks, and cameo appearances from other urban fantasies' characters.... Lush and fun." —*Kirkus Reviews*

"Trust us, you'll be so into this smart, funny, romantic read that you won't even be frustrated at the cliff-hanger ending—we're just counting down to 2009, when the final chapter in Clary's story hits the shelves!" —*Cosmo Girl*

The Infernal Devices

"Compulsively readable, this is the first title in a new, companion series set 100 years earlier than the author's bestselling Mortal Instruments books.

Packed with battles, romantic entanglements, and tantalizing foreshadowing, this will have readers clamoring for the next installment. Although prior knowledge of the Mortal Instruments books isn't necessary to enjoy this title, you can bet your sword newcomers to the world will be rushing to read what they've missed."—*Booklist*

"Methodically researched, [Clare's] Victorian London is dark and romantic, and the strong-willed Tessa is an unexpected hero readers will love. . . . At completion, the reader has more questions than answers, but the clarity of writing and quick plot turns will ensure its popularity."—*VOYA*

"The events often read as bleakly as the Victorian London weather, punctuated by Clare's trademark humor, empathy, and authentic characters, who fight their own flaws and tragic pasts as often as they do evil. Mysteries, misdirection, and riddles abound, and while there are some gruesome moments, they never feel gratuitous. Fans of the Mortal Instruments series and newcomers alike won't be disappointed."—*Publishers Weekly*

"Readers will be thrilled and amazed with this prequel to the Mortal Instruments, tearing their way through a beautifully constructed story of action, magic, mayhem and romance. Fans and newcomers alike will be enchanted by Clare's fantastical world and left begging for more!" —*Romantic Times*

"Vampires, warlocks, demons, and steampunk elements such as clockwork monstrosities abound in this supernatural offering. From the erratic and volatile—yet charming—Will, to the bumbling and amiable inventor, Henry, to the ethereal and gentle Jem, Clare has made each character unique. The action-heavy plot takes off from the first page, propelling readers toward a dramatic conclusion." —*School Library Journal*

1973 Judith Rumelt is born in Tehran, Iran.

2004 Cassandra Clare's first fiction sale, a short story titled "The Girl's Guide to Defeating the Dark Lord," is published in the *Turn the Other Chick* anthology.

2004 Cassandra Clare begins work on *City of Bones*, her first novel in the Mortal Instruments series.

2007 *City of Bones* is published, earning best-seller status and numerous awards. Subsequent novels in the Mortal Instruments series are published between 2008 and 2014.

2010 Clare marries Josh Lewis.

2010 *Clockwork Angel*, the first novel in the Infernal Devices series, is published, followed by *Clockwork Prince* in 2011, and *Clockwork Princess* in 2013.

2013 The movie *Mortal Instruments: City of Bones* is released.

2013 "What Really Happened in Peru," the first of a ten-part series of short works featuring the character of Magnus Bane, is published. The Bane Chronicles series, cowritten with two of Clare's author friends, concludes in 2014, and a compiled edition is published in print.

2014 *The Iron Trial*, the first novel in the five-part Magisterium series cowritten with Holly Black, is published.

2014 *Walker Books acquires the United Kingdom, Australian, New Zealand, and export rights to the Last Hours. Set in 1903 in London and Paris, the new series will be a sequel to the Infernal Devices.*

2015 *Lady Midnight*, the first novel in the three-part series the Dark Artifices, is published.

GLOSSARY

ALADDIN Famous character in a Middle Eastern folk tale.

AMATEUR One who excels at a skill such as writing but does not use it to earn money.

ANACHRONISTIC Not in keeping with the times, such as using modern terms in historical fiction.

ANTHOLOGY Collection of literary works.

ANTIQUATED Old-fashioned or out of style.

CAMEO Brief or minor role of a character in a literary or theatrical/film production.

CASTING Selecting actors to portray specific characters.

CHOCOLATE GELT Chocolate candy molded as coins, common at Jewish Chanukah festivities.

CHRONICLES Descriptions of specific sequences of events.

CODEX A text usually of Scripture, great works, or ancient chronicles.

COMIC RELIEF The unexpected injection of humor into a tense scene.

COPYRIGHT LAW Law defining under what terms an author's published work may be reproduced by others.

COUNTERFEITING Making imitations of money or other valuables.

DEMONOLOGY Study of evil spirits.

DREYDL Four-sided spinning top used in a Jewish gambling game; also spelled dreidel.

FAERIE Supernatural spirit who causes mischief.

GARAGE BAND Amateur rock group typically rehearsing in a garage or basement and performing for friends.

GENETICS Science dealing with heredity.

GENRE Form of literature, such as fantasy, mystery, historical, or romance; musical genres include heavy metal, folk, rap, country, jazz, blues, etc.

GRAPHIC NOVEL Novel reproduced in comic book format.

IDIOMS Language or dialect spoken by a certain group of people.

MECHANICAL ENGINEER Professional who designs and maintains machinery and tools.

MILIEU Someone's social surroundings.

MYTHOLOGY Legends concerning gods and extraordinary heroes and heroines in an ancient culture.

NEMESIS Constant and particularly formidable rival.

PENCHANT A liking or enjoyment of something or inclination to act a certain way.

PHRASEOLOGY The way words are organized into phrases.

POTATO LATKE Type of fried potato pancake popular in the Jewish Chanukah tradition.

PREQUEL Book or series that is set in time before the first-published book or series.

PROTAGONIST Main character.

RUNE Ancient alphabetic character with mysterious meaning.

SCREENING Showing of a film to a select audience before its general release.

SEQUEL Book or series that continues the plot or theme of its predecessor.

STEAMPUNK A genre of science fiction that usually features steam-powered machines instead of advanced technology.

TRANCE MUSIC Genre of electronic dance music evoking a hypnotic sensation.

TRILOGY Three-part literary work.

TUTOR Private teacher.

VAMPIRE Supernatural character who sucks blood from humans.

WARLOCK Person who practices black magic.

WEREWOLF Person who can assume the form of a wolf.

American Folklore Society
Mershon Center
Ohio State University
1501 Neil Avenue
Columbus, OH 43201-2602
(614) 292-4715
Website: http://www.afsnet.org
This society is devoted to studying lore and legends
    of national and world cultures.

American Library Association (ALA)
50 E. Huron Street
Chicago, IL 60611-2795
(800) 545-2433
Website: http://www.ala.org
The ALA provides resources for librarians and other
    members. Its Young Adult Library Services
    Association (YALSA) division has named
    several of Clare's novels to its Teens Top Ten
    Awards lists.

Canadian Authors Association
6 West Street N, Suite 203
Orillia, ON L3V 5B8
Canada
(866) 216-6222
Website: http://canadianauthors.org
The association offers resources and programs for
    aspiring writers as well as published
    professionals.

Children's Book Council
54 W. 39th Street, 14th Floor
New York, NY 10018
(212) 966-1990
Website: http://www.cbcbooks.org
The Children's Book Council is a national association of
children's book publishers. It named *Clockwork
Prince* Teen Book of the Year in 2012.

International Fantasy Gaming Society
P.O. Box 36555
Cincinnati, OH 45236
Website: http://www.ifgs.org
This society produces live role-playing events with
fantasy themes. Games are for all ages and fea-
ture role-playing, safe ("boffer") combat, and
teamwork, as well as costume and prop making.

International Reading Association
P.O. Box 8139
Newark, DE 19714-8139
(800) 336-7323
Website: http://www.reading.org
The International Reading Association is a world-
wide network of organizations and individuals
committed to literacy. It named *City of Ashes*
a Young Adults Choice title in 2010.

Los Angeles Science Fantasy Society
6012 Tyrone Avenue

Van Nuys, CA 91404
(818) 904-9544
Website: http://lasfs.org
The LASFS, founded in 1934, is said to be "this
world's oldest continuously active science-
fiction and fantasy club." Open to visitors, it
meets weekly and sponsors discussions,
events, and projects.

New Atlantic Independent Booksellers Association
2667 Hyacinth Street
Westbury, NY 11590
(516) 333.0681
Website: http://www.naiba.com
This is an organization of independently owned book-
stores. Its best-seller lists have included
Clockwork Angel.

Science Fiction & Fantasy Writers of America
P.O. Box 3238
Enfield, CT 06083-3238
Website: http://www.sfwa.org
This professional organization for authors of science and fantasy fiction and similar genres
"informs, supports, promotes, defends and
advocates for its members." It provides
numerous resources for novice authors.

SF Canada
7433 East River Road

Washago, ON L0K 2B0
Canada
Website: http://www.sfcanada.org
SF Canada is a Canadian association for writers of
"speculative fiction"—science fiction, fantasy,
horror "and any other weird fiction that
invokes a sense of wonder."

WEBSITES

Because of the changing nature of Internet links,
Rosen Publishing has developed an online list of
websites related to the subject of this book. This site
is updated regularly. Please use this link to access
the list:

http://www.rosenlinks.com/AAA/Clare

Allan, Tony, and Sara Maitland. *Ancient Greece and Rome: Myths and Beliefs.* New York, NY: Rosen Publishing Group, 2011.

Bellanger, Michelle. *The Dictionary of Demons: Names of the Damned.* Woodbury, MN: Llewellyn Publications, 2010.

Black, Holly. *Doll Bones.* New York, NY: Margaret K. McElderry Books (Simon & Schuster Books for Young Readers), 2013.

Brennan, Sarah Rees. *Unspoken* (The Lynburn Legacy). New York, NY: Random House Books for Young Readers, 2012.

Bringle, Jennifer. *Vampires in Film and Television.* New York, NY: Rosen Central, 2011.

Clare, Cassandra, and Joshua Lewis. *The Shadowhunter's Codex: Being a Record of the Ways and Laws of the Nephilim, the Chosen of the Angel Raziel.* New York, NY: Simon & Schuster Books for Young Readers, 2013.

Cohen, Robert Z. *Transylvania: Birthplace of Vampires.* New York, NY: Rosen Central, 2011.

Curran, Bob. *Werewolves: A Field Guide to Shapeshifters, Lycanthropes, and Man-Beasts.* Pompton Plains, NJ: New Page Books, 2012.

Gerani, Gary. *Top 100 Fantasy Movies.* San Diego, CA: IDW Publishing, 2013.

Gresh, Lois H. *The Mortal Instruments Companion: City of Bones, Shadowhunters, and the Sight: The Unauthorized Guide.* New York, NY: St. Martin's Griffin, 2013.

Hanley, Victoria. *Seize the Story: A Handbook for Teens Who Like to Write.* Waco, TX: Prufrock Press, 2011.

Hindu Mythology. San Diego, CA: Lucent Books, 2014.

Indovino, Saina C. *Dracula and Beyond: Famous Vampires & Werewolves in Literature and Film.* Broomall, PA: Mason Crest Publishers, 2010.

Johnson, Maureen. *The Name of the Star.* New York, NY: Penguin Group USA, 2011.

Kallen, Stuart A. *Vampire History and Lore.* San Diego, CA: Referencepoint Press, 2010.

Lamson, Laurie. *Now Write! Science Fiction, Fantasy, and Horror.* New York, NY: Jeremy P. Tarcher/ Penguin, 2014.

MacDonald, Fiona. *Vampires: A Very Peculiar History.* Brighton, England: Book House (Salariya Book Company), 2010.

Mack, Carol K., and Dinah Mack. *A Field Guide to Demons, Vampires, Fallen Angels and Other Subversive Spirits.* New York, NY: Arcade Publishing (Skyhorse Publishing), 2011.

Meyer, Stephenie. *The Twilight Saga: The Complete Illustrated Guide.* New York, NY: Little, Brown Books for Young Readers, 2011.

Nardo, Don. *Roman Mythology.* San Diego, CA: Lucent Books (Thomson-Gale), 2012.

O'Connor, Mimi. *Shadowhunter's Guide: City of Bones (The Mortal Instruments).* New York, NY: Margaret K. McElderry Books, 2013.

Ouyang, Wen-chin, ed. *The Arabian Nights.* New York, NY: Everyman's Library (Random House), 2014.

Schomp, Virginia. *The City* (Life in Victorian England). Salt Lake City, UT: Benchmark Books, 2010.

Spencer, Liv. *Navigating the Shadow World: The Unofficial Guide to Cassandra Clare's The Mortal Instruments.* Toronto, ON: ECW Press, 2013.

Stewart, Gail B. *Victorian England.* San Diego, CA: Referencepoint Press, 2013.

Triggs, Teal. *Fanzines: The DIY Revolution.* San Francisco, CA: Chronicle Books, 2010.

Werner, Alex, and Tony Williams. *Dickens's Victorian London: 1839–1901.* London, England: Ebury Press/Random House, 2012.

Woog, Adam. *Vampires in the Movies* (Vampire Library). San Diego, CA: Referencepoint Press, 2010.

Wukovits, John F. *The Victorian Era* (World History). San Diego, CA: Lucent Books (Thomson-Gale), 2013.

BIBLIOGRAPHY

Alter, Alexandra. "The New Queen of Fantasy: Cassandra Clare's Breakout." *Wall Street Journal*, June 15, 2012. Retrieved December 2013 (http://online.wsj.com/news/articles/SB1000142405270230373420457746459 3388416630).

Alter, Alexandra. "The Weird World of Fan Fiction." *Wall Street Journal*, June 14, 2012. Retrieved February 2014 (http://online.wsj.com/news/articles/SB100014240527023037342045774 6 4411825970488).

Barraclough, Leo. "'Mortal Instruments: City of Ashes' Set to Shoot in 2014." *Variety*, October 23, 2013. Retrieved February 2014 (http://variety.com/2013/film/international/mortal -instruments-city-of-ashes-set-to-shoot-in -2014-1200754848).

Bookish Type. "Author Interview: Cassandra Clare (The Infernal Devices & The Mortal Instruments)." August 16, 2010. Retrieved January 2014 (http://thebookishtype.blogspot.com/2010/08/author -interview-cassandra-clare.html).

Brody, Cheryl. "Cassandra Clare." *Seventeen*, 2014. Retrieved January 2014 (http://www .seventeen.com/entertainment/features/ city-of-ashes-cassandra-clare).

CassandraClare.com. "Cassandra Clare, *New York Times* Bestselling Author." Retrieved December 2013–March 2014 (http://www .cassandraclare.com).

Eyre, Charlotte. "Walker Acquires New Cassandra Clare Trilogy." *The Bookseller*, February 21, 2014. Retrieved March 2014 (http://www.thebookseller.com/news/walker-acquires-new-cassandra-clare-trilogy.html).

Freitas, Donna. "Q&A with Cassandra Clare." *Publishers Weekly*, March 5, 2009. Retrieved January 2014 (http://www.publishersweekly.com/pw/by-topic/authors/interviews/article/12364-q-a-with-cassandra-clare.html).

Hayman, Stacey. "Wouldn't You Like to Know . . . Cassandra Clare." *Voya*, March 9, 2012. Retrieved March 2014 (http://www.voyamagazine.com/2012/03/09/wouldnt-you-like-to-know-cassandra-clare).

Kaplan, David A. "A Most Unusual Father-Daughter Professional Pairing." *Fortune* blog, August 29, 2012. Retrieved January 2014 (http://features.blogs.fortune.cnn.com/2012/08/29/cassandra-clare-richard-rumelt/?section=magazines_fortune).

Kit, Borys. "Sigourney Weaver in Talks to Join 'Mortal Instruments: City of Ashes' (Exclusive)." *Hollywood Reporter*, July 29, 2013. Retrieved January 2014 (http://www.hollywoodreporter.com/heat-vision/sigourney-weaver-talks-join-mortal-594995).

Melendez, Blanca. "Q&A: Cassandra Clare on 'The Mortal Instruments.'" *ArtsBeat* blog, *New York Times*, August 27, 2013. Retrieved January

2014 (http://artsbeat.blogs.nytimes
.com/2013/08/27/q-a-cassandra-clare-talks
-about-the-mortal-instruments/?_php
=true&_type=blogs&_r=0).

Metro.us. "Putting the Hard Sell on Steampunk."
October 25, 2010. Retrieved January 2014
(http://www.metro.us/boston/entertainment/
books/2010/10/25/putting-the-hard-sell-on
-steampunk).

Pon, Cindy. "Interview with Cassandra Clare."
Enchanted Inkpot, November 2, 2010.
Retrieved January 2014 (http://enchantedinkpot
.livejournal.com/72742.html).

Powell's Books. "Kids' Q&A: Cassandra Clare."
Retrieved January 2014 (http://www.powells
.com/kidsqa/clare.html).

Rooney, Chandra, ed. "Top 10 of 2010: Teen
Fiction." *Indigo Teen.* Retrieved January 2014
(http://blog.indigo.ca/teen/item/160-top-10-of
-2010.html).

Schillaci, Sophie. "'Mortal Instruments': How
Author Cassandra Clare Helped Bring the
Book to Life." *Hollywood Reporter*, August
20, 2013. Retrieved January 2014 (http://
www.hollywoodreporter.com/news/mortal
-instruments-how-author-cassandra-609043).

Smith, Cynthia Leitich. "Author Interview:
Cassandra Clare on City of Bones (Book One,
The Mortal Instruments)." *Cynsations*, March
8, 2008. Retrieved January 2014 (http://

cynthialeitichsmith.blogspot.com/2008/
03/author-interview-cassandra-clare-on.html).
3 Evil Cousins "Cassandra Clare, Author Extraordinaire,
Answers Our 13 Evil Questions." March 13, 2008.
Retrieved January 2014 (http://3evilcousins
.blogspot.com/2008/03/cassandra-clare-author
-extrordanaire.html).
Walsh, Adele. "Interview: Cassandra Clare."
Persnickety Snark, March 18, 2009. Retrieved
January 2014 (http://www.persnicketysnark
.com/2009/03/interview-cassandra-clare.html).

INDEX

ABOUT THE AUTHOR

Daniel E. Harmon is the author of more than ninety books on topics ranging from world exploration to international studies. His historical mystery fiction works include two short story series, *The Harper Chronicles* and *The Casebook of MacTavish*. A career writer and editor, he has contributed articles to scores of magazines and newspapers. He lives in Spartanburg, South Carolina.

PHOTO CREDITS

Cover, p. 3 Frederic J. Brown/AFP/Getty Images; p. 7 Eric Charbonneau/Invision/AP Images; p. 10 diane10981/iStock/Thinkstock; pp. 12–13 Kim Carson/Digital Vision/Thinkstock; p. 17 The Bridgeman Art Library/Getty Images; p. 19 Culture Club/Hulton Archive/Getty Images; pp. 22–23 John Shearer/Invision/AP Images; p. 25 © Entertainment Pictures/ZUMA Press; pp. 28–29 Rafy/©Screen Gems/courtesy Everett Collection; pp. 33, 36, 43 Jonathan Leibson/Getty Images; pp. 38–39 © Sony Pictures/Entertainment Pictures/ZUMA Press; p. 46 Sean Pavone/Shuttesrstock.com; pp. 50–51 boboling/iStock/Thinkstock; pp. 54–55 Hulton Archive/Getty Images; p. 63 Frazer Harrison/Getty Images; pp. 66–67 Rex Features/AP Images; p. 70 Paul Archuleta/FilmMagic/Getty Images; p. 73 Tom Grill/The Image Bank/Getty Images; p. 78 Europa Press/Getty Images; pp. 82–83 Lisa Lake/Getty Images; cover, back cover, interior pages (book) © www.istockphoto.com/ Andrzej Tokarski; cover, back cover, interior pages (background pattern) javarman/Shutterstock.com; interior pages background image (textured wall and fence) © iStockphoto.com/cpurser.

Designer: Nicole Russo; Editor: Heather Moore Niver; Photo Researcher: Marty Levick